FORTS OF CANADA

Written by
Ann-Maureen Owens
and Jane Yealland

Illustrated by
Don Kilby

Kids Can Press

To Brian, Luke, David and Kevin — AMO
To Alex, Jill, Carly and Christopher — JY

Acknowledgements

We would like to express our appreciation to the curators, historians and staff at fort sites across Canada who answered our many questions and provided us with their unique insights. In particular we would like to thank Carl Benn of Fort York; Jim Candow, John Grenville and Bill Yeo of Canadian Heritage; D.J. Delaney of Fort Wellington; Adrienne Gardner of Sainte-Marie among the Hurons; Tammy Hannibal of the Hudson Bay Company Archives; Nicole Herod of Artillery Park, Quebec City; Rebecca Holland of Fort Whoop-Up; Stephen Mecredy of Fort Henry; Marty Mascarin of Fort William; Bill McKie of the RCMP Centennial Museum; David Newhouse, Paul Bourgeoise and Edna Manitowabi of the Native Studies Department at Trent University; Nicole Ouellet of Fort No. 1, Point Lévis; Rose Anne Poirier of the Fortress of Louisbourg; and Janne Switzer of Fort Edmonton.

We are also grateful for the advice and suggestions of Mary Beaty, Joanne Breadner, David Graham, Pamela Hodgson, Brian Owens, Peter Owens, Gerald Penney, Ken Stewart and Alex Yealland. As well, many thanks to our friends and families for their moral support.

A big thank you for testing the activities in the book to the enthusiastic students of St. Paul Catholic School, Kingston; Winston Churchill Public School, Kingston; the Kingfest Summer Enrichment Courses; and of course our own children. Special thanks are also due to our publishers, Valerie Hussey and Ricky Englander; illustrator, Don Kilby; book designer, Karen Powers; and especially to our very skilled and patient editor, Elizabeth MacLeod.

Kids Can Press acknowledges the financial support of the Ontario Arts Council, the Canada Council for the Arts and the Government of Canada, through the BPIDP, for our publishing activity.

Published in Canada by
Kids Can Press Ltd.
29 Birch Avenue
Toronto, ON M4V 1E2

Published in the U.S. by
Kids Can Press Ltd.
2250 Military Road
Tonawanda, NY 14150

Edited by Elizabeth MacLeod
Designed by Karen Powers
Printed and bound in Canada by Kromar Printing

CM 96 0 9 8 7 6 5 4 3 2 1
CM PA 96 0 9 8 7 6 5 4 3

Canadian Cataloguing in Publication Data

Owens, Ann-Maureen
  Forts of Canada

Includes index.
ISBN 1-55074-316-3 (bound)   ISBN 1-55074-271-X (pbk.)

1. Fortification — Canada — History — Juvenile literature.
2. Battles — Canada — Juvenile literature. I. Yealland, Jane.
II. Kilby, Don. III. Title.

UG413.O84 1995   j355.7'0971   C95-932429-1

Kids Can Press is a Nelvana company

CONTENTS

Have you ever built a fort?

Have you ever piled up a barricade of cushions, hammered pieces of scrap wood up in a tree or stacked snowballs for protection in a snowball fight? If the answer is yes, then you already know something about building forts.

Forts have been built all over the world by people who wanted to defend themselves. In North America, chiefs of Aboriginal peoples surrounded their villages with wooden palisades, and kings in other parts of the world built castles. Most Canadian forts — there were more than 200 — were built from the early 1600s until the late 1800s.

Like the castles of Europe, the forts of Canada became today's cities and towns. Where you live now could have been the site of a fort long ago. Some places are still called by their fort names,

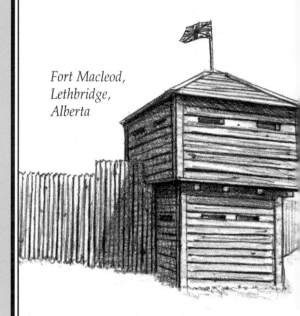

Fort Macleod, Lethbridge, Alberta

such as Fort Erie in Ontario, Fort Simpson in the Northwest Territories and Fort Macleod in Alberta.

Carleton Martello Tower, Saint John, New Brunswick

Fort Lennox,
Île-aux-Noix, Quebec

Nils von Schoultz, the ghost of
Fort Henry, Kingston, Ontario

Some forts have been repaired or rebuilt to look the way they did when they were used long ago. If you visit one of these forts, look for secret tunnels, deadly cannons and even a few ghosts from the days when forts were the most important places in Canada.

Read on to find out about many different Canadian forts, what it was like to live in one and how you can make models of some of those forts. If you come across any fort words you don't understand, look them up in the glossary on page 63.

Many large cities — including Halifax, Montreal, Toronto and Calgary — still have a fort in among their skyscrapers and expressways.

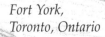

Fort York,
Toronto, Ontario

CHAPTER ONE

FIRST FORTS
Survival in the wilderness

I f you could travel 400 years or more back in time, you would find no cities, no farms and no roads in Canada — only endless trees, clear streams, plenty of wild animals and people building forts so they could feel safe.

These first forts had three things in common:
1. They were simple wooden structures.
2. They could be built quickly.
3. They helped people survive the fierce cold of Canada's winter storms and the dangers that lurked in the forests.

In this chapter you will find out how some Aboriginal people (the Native people of Canada) built their forts, how a man called Champlain designed the first European fort in Canada and how a 14-year-old girl saved a fort from attack.

Aboriginal village forts

The Huron and Iroquois Nations who lived during the 1400s in the area now called Ontario and Quebec designed their villages as forts surrounded by a wall of tree trunks. The wall was called a palisade and was built in a circle so it could guard against attack in any direction. This was necessary because young men often attacked each other's villages to prove their bravery.

To make the palisade, Aboriginal people used stone axes to chop down trees about 5 to 7 m (16 to 23 ft.) tall. Then they trimmed the tree trunks and sunk them into the ground so they were upright and close together circling the longhouses of the village. Flexible saplings were woven between the poles — much like a basket is woven — to fill in any gaps. This made the palisade strong enough to withstand the enemies' arrows and spears.

To prevent attackers from getting close enough to chop through the palisade with hatchets or burn it down with torches, a young boy kept guard in a lookout tree. At his warning yell, the women working in the cornfields around the village ran for the safety of the palisade and squeezed through its narrow gateway. The men inside the palisade shot arrows and hurled stones from a raised platform, while women threw birch-bark pails full of water on any flaming arrows that hit the palisade.

You'll need
- a package of brown Plasticine or other modelling clay
- a piece of stiff cardboard about 50 cm x 50 cm (20 in. x 20 in.)
- about 75 twigs 15 cm (6 in.) long and one 20 cm (8 in.) long
- 2 cardboard bathroom tissue rolls
- a sheet of 23 cm x 30 cm (9 in. x 12 in.) brown construction paper, torn into 2.5 cm x 2.5 cm (1 in. x 1 in.) squares
- scissors, glue

1. Set aside a small piece of clay for step 4. Roll the rest into a snake 1 m (3 ft.) long and about 2 cm (¾ in.) thick. Shape it into a circle on the cardboard, leaving a 10-cm (4-in.) opening, as shown. Glue the clay in place and allow the glue to dry.

2. Stick the 75 twigs upright in the clay, 0.5 cm (¼ in.) apart, to form the wooden palisade.

3. To make a longhouse, slit a bathroom tissue roll lengthwise and open it into a U. Poke smokeholes in the top, as shown. To cover the longhouse with bark shingles, glue the brown squares all over it but not over the smokeholes. Repeat for the second longhouse.

4. Use the clay you set aside in step 1 to anchor the longer twig at the palisade opening for a lookout tree.

5. Place the longhouses inside the palisade. Add whatever details you like according to what you see on pages 6 and 7.

Home sweet fort: the habitations

M arc puts down his axe and wearily wipes the sweat from his face. Then a chilly wind reminds him why he and his friends are hurrying to finish their new home at Port Royal, Nova Scotia. Last winter on Ste-Croix Island, not far from this spot, half of his companions died of cold, hunger and a disease called scurvy. Marc learned later that scurvy is caused by going for a long time without fresh vegetables and fruit, which were in short supply last year.

Marc hopes the winter of 1605 will be different. His leader, Samuel de Champlain, has made friends with the Micmacs, who gave him their cure for scurvy. It involves boiling spruce needles and tastes terrible, but it works.

Champlain has also drawn up plans for what he calls a habitation. It will be a square fort with tiny windows facing the river and two bastions, or lookout towers, on the corners that face inland. Marc and the other men have chopped down many trees and built four buildings for the bedrooms, kitchen and dining room that all face each other across a courtyard. A well in the courtyard provides plenty of fresh water, and some rooms even have stone fireplaces for cooking and warmth.

Marc is looking forward to the parties that Champlain's new club, the Order of Good Cheer, has planned. Every week one member of the group has to gather food for a feast as well as entertain the others. "Perhaps," Marc tells a friend, "I'll put on a short play when it is my turn. I hope it pleases the members of the club, especially Champlain."

BRAVE MADELEINE

Madeleine de Verchères was just 14 years old when she was forced to defend her home, a small fort like the habitations. In October 1692, while both her parents were away, about 45 Iroquois suddenly attacked. Madeleine was frightened, but she quickly passed out guns and ammunition to her two younger brothers and a few servants. They moved along the wall as they fired their muskets and shouted, "All's well!" That made the Iroquois think the fort was well guarded. Madeleine's leadership kept everyone going for eight days until help arrived. For her bravery, she received a reward from the King of France.

Port Royal

11

Forts of the Black Robes

Aboriginal people called the French Jesuit priests "Black Robes" because of the long, dark robes they wore. The Black Robes built mission forts throughout Canada during the 1600s. Of these, Sainte-Marie among the Hurons, on Georgian Bay in Ontario, was the largest. Unlike the circular Huron and Iroquois forts, Sainte-Marie's palisades were built with metal axes and in the rectangular style of European estates.

The mission fort also had lookout towers called bastions, which allowed a sentry to guard two walls at once.

People had different opinions about missionaries and mission forts.

NATIVE AREA

Sainte-Marie among the Hurons

PRIEST:

"I came to convert the Hurons to Christianity. Fort Sainte-Marie was built in 1639 as a safe home where I could pray and teach. Unfortunately, the Hurons' enemies, the Iroquois, became my enemies too. I never fought them, though other Frenchmen did."

HURON:

"The Black Robes came in peace but they brought terrible diseases with them. And the Iroquois increased attacks on us after we welcomed the Black Robes. The Black Robes shared their iron tools with us and we showed them how to grow corn, beans and squash."

1. Five-sided Bastion
2. Longhouse
3. Hospital
4. Wigwam
5. Cemetery
6. Church of St. Joseph
7. "En Colombage"
8. Shoemaker-Tailor Shop
9. "En Pilier"
10. Waterway
11. Blacksmith Shop
12. Carpenter Shop
13. Chapel
14. Jesuit Residence
15. Stables
16. Cookhouse
17. Farmer's Dwelling
18. Cookhouse Garden
19. Boivin Building
20. Granary
21. Bastion
22. Wood Storage and Barracks

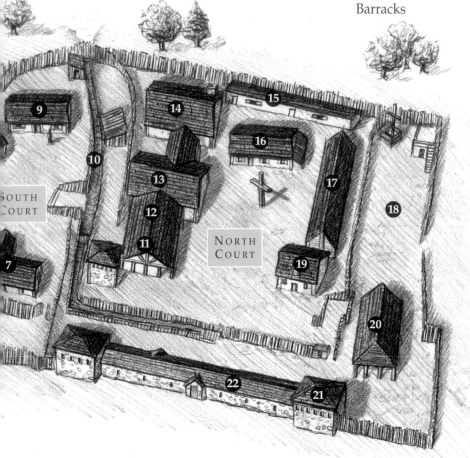

SOUTH COURT

NORTH COURT

IROQUOIS:

"My people were the most powerful when the French came. The French sent the Hurons into our hunting grounds to get beaver pelts for them. The French used guns against us, but now our people have guns from the Dutch and the English."

CHRISTMAS, 1641

Have you ever sung the beautiful song called the Huron Christmas Carol? Did you know it was written more than 350 years ago? Father Jean de Brébeuf, who lived at Sainte-Marie among the Hurons, wrote it to tell the Huron people about Christmas. He became fluent in the Huron language, which is a difficult language to learn. For instance, there's a Huron sound not found in the French language. Father Brébeuf used the number 8 to represent it. In Huron the song he wrote is called "Jesous Ahatonnia" and the first line is "Estennislon de tson8e Iesg8s ahatonnia," which is sung in English as " 'Twas in the moon of winter time when all the birds had fled."

CHAPTER TWO

GUARDIANS OF THE SHORE

I t's been weeks since you left France to sail to Canada and your food is almost gone. Will you ever see land again? Suddenly the watchman cries, "Land ho!" and you rush to the deck rail to see the stone walls and wooden towers of the Fortress of Louisbourg as they slowly come into view.

Along the east coast of Canada in the 1700s, large stone coastal forts replaced the smaller, less-permanent wooden ones because more soldiers, settlers and traders were coming to stay. Britain and France also built these more permanent coastal forts because they could withstand the harsh winter storms and protect the people inside from the cannon fire of enemy ships.

Read on to find out more about pirates, secret signals and how to make your own mini-coastal fort.

How forts battle warships

Forts have two weaknesses when they are attacked by warships. First, they can't be moved, so they're sitting targets for ships' cannon fire. And second, when food or ammunition runs low, warships can block a fort's supply lines. This is called a blockade.

Fort builders tried many tactics to overcome these weaknesses. In the 1700s, the French created fortresses by building walls around entire towns. See page 18 to find out more about them.

The British defended their important harbours by building a series of small forts to protect each other. For example, before enemy ships could reach the Citadel, Halifax's main fort, they would have to get past gun blasts and cannon fire from a series of smaller forts. Some of these forts were built on islands in the harbour, while others, such as York Redoubt, sat on the highest coastal cliffs so they gave soldiers a good view of incoming ships.

One specialized harbour defence the British used was a mini-fort called a Martello tower. The tower's flat roof was equipped with a large cannon mounted on a circular track so it could swing around to fire in any direction. Some towers were protected from snow and rain by a pointed roof that could be removed when the cannon was needed. Between 1796 and 1846, the British built Carleton Martello Tower at Saint John, New Brunswick, as well as towers at Halifax, Nova Scotia; Quebec City, Quebec; and Kingston, Ontario.

The Citadel was first built as a wooden stockade in 1749. Its main purpose was to oppose the nearby French Fortress of Louisbourg. Over the years it was rebuilt as a stone fort.

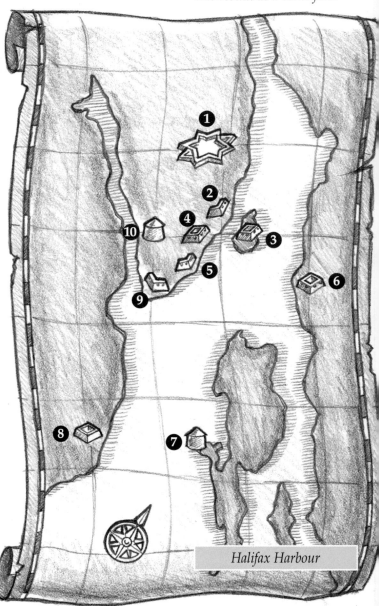

Halifax Harbour

1. Citadel
2. Grand Battery
3. Fort Charlotte
4. Fort Ogilvie
5. Point Pleasant Battery
6. Fort Clarence
7. Sherbrooke Tower
8. York Redoubt
9. Northwest Arms Battery
10. Prince of Wales Tower

You'll need
- a round 2 L (2 qt.) ice cream container

- a piece of thick cardboard 30 cm x 40 cm (12 in. x 16 in.)

- 250 mL (1 c.) water

- 250 mL (1 c.) flour

- 10 pages of newspaper cut into strips 30 cm x 5 cm (12 in. x 2 in.)

- a sheet of black construction paper

- masking tape, scissors, water-based paints and a paintbrush

1. Remove the lid from the ice cream container and put it aside. Turn the container upside-down and tape it to the cardboard.

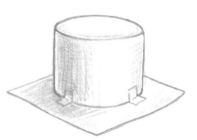

2. Mix together the water and flour until they form a smooth paste.

3. Dip each newspaper strip into the paste and lay it on the container.

4. Cover the top and sides with two layers of strips. Be sure to cover the tape too. Leave the tower to dry overnight.

5. Paint the tower grey. When it's dry, add details such as white lines to look like mortar between bricks and a black door and windows. Paint the base blue if your tower is surrounded by water or green and brown if it is on the coast.

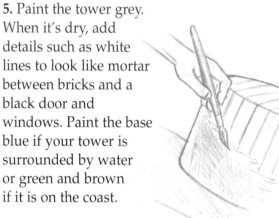

6. To make the roof, place the lid of the ice cream container on the black paper and trace around it. Cut out the circle. Then cut a straight line into its centre. Shape it into a cone for the roof. Tape it to the top of the tower so its edge extends beyond the tower's walls.

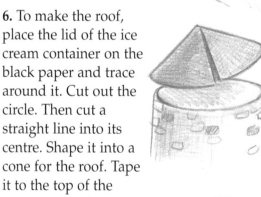

7. Add details such as a flag and a cannon, if you like.

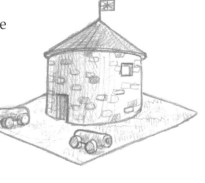

The fortress: more than a fort

The Fortress of Louisbourg

By the 1700s the French were protecting their most important coastal settlements by enclosing them with walls to make fortresses. A fortress is a walled town that can be defended. For instance, the French began building Louisbourg in 1716 for soldiers as well as for more than 3000 men, women and children, who were fishermen, merchants, artisans, innkeepers, schoolchildren — there was even an astronomer!

More than 20 years of work and about $240 million in today's money went into building the Fortress of Louisbourg. It was said to be the strongest fortress of its day and was one of France's main trading centres. Seven hundred French soldiers guarded Louisbourg's high walls. They had more than 100 cannons, which they fired through small openings, called embrassures, in the walls. Sound impossible to capture? The British did it twice, in 1745 and 1758, by blocking the harbour and stopping food from reaching the fortress inhabitants. Louisbourg had to surrender both times.

The Fortress of Quebec guarded another important French harbour. Quebec was a vital shipping and loading port because big ships could not sail up the St. Lawrence River past this point — the river becomes too narrow. The fortress was involved in many battles, and the one that took place there in 1759 decided Canada's future. After firing his ships' cannons at the fortress for two months, the British commander, General Wolfe, managed to land his soldiers on its west side, blocking any escape to the nearest French settlement, Montreal. The French leader, General Montcalm, realized that his fortress would soon be under siege, so he sent his army out to fight on the Plains of Abraham. The British won the battle and New France became known as British North America.

The Fortress of Quebec

TRADITIONAL GAMES

Children in eighteenth-century Louisbourg and Quebec didn't have many toys or much time for fun. But they did enjoy playing games, including these two they learned from Aboriginal children.

SNAKE

This is a winter game. You and your friend each choose a stick about 1 m (3 ft.) long. Take turns shooting your sticks along an icy patch of ground. If your stick goes the farthest, you win.

DUCK-ON-A-ROCK

Organize your friends into two teams and choose a large, flat place to be the "bowling alley." Place a small rock on top of a larger rock at one end of the bowling alley. Stand 4.5 m (15 ft.) away and imagine the top rock is a duck. Each team member takes a turn standing at the far end of the alley and carefully throwing a rock underhand at the duck. If you hit the duck you score a point. Make lots of noise when the other team throws the rock. Players long ago pretended this would distract the rock from hitting the duck.

Keeping in touch

Without telephones or loudspeakers, special signals were needed to communicate inside forts and from fort to fort. Within fort walls, signals that you could hear were used. Boys as young as 12 years old played these signals on drums or a type of flute called a fife. Some tunes told the troops when to get up, others announced mealtimes. Other tunes were played loudly enough to let the soldiers know what to do next during a noisy battle.

To communicate between forts, you had to use signals that people could see. In the 1780s at some coastal forts, signal flags told the townspeople if a storm was coming or which ship was arriving in the harbour. You used a different set of flags to send military messages using secret codes. You could also communicate with ships by using the semaphore signal code during the day and a flashing light code at night. By the late 1800s the telegraph began to replace flag signals.

PRINCE EDWARD: ROYAL FORT COMMANDER

When Prince Edward became commander-in-chief of the fort in Halifax in 1794, he immediately faced a tough challenge. France had just declared war on Britain, so Edward had to prepare the Citadel for battle. Ramparts and bastions were built around the fort, as well as a shallow ditch with a row of sharp-pointed palisades.

Edward insisted that his soldiers always be on time. So he had a clock tower erected at the Citadel — you can still tell time by the clock today. He also invented the Citadel's flag signal system to send secret messages to soldiers in outlying forts. Prince Edward returned to England in 1828 but he's still remembered here — Prince Edward Island is named after him.

Semaphore is a way to send a message to a friend who is too far away to hear you but can still see you. You make each letter of the alphabet by positioning your arms as shown in the chart below. If you hold small flags made out of sticks and paper, your friend can see your message from an even greater distance.

A	B	C
D	E	F
G	H	I
J	K	L
M	N	O
P	Q	R
S	T	U
V	W	X
Y	Z	ERROR

Seafarers' forts

If you sailed from Europe to Canada, the first place you could land would be Newfoundland. For centuries people from Europe landed there and built many different types of forts. Fishermen from England, France, Holland, Spain and Portugal built temporary forts along Newfoundland's coast to protect themselves from pirates.

There were even pirate forts! Peter Easton, Newfoundland's most famous pirate captain, built his fort at Harbour Grace around 1600 so he would have a place to hide after he attacked ships.

In 1673, in the place where St. John's stands today, an English fishing captain and his 22 sailors dragged their ship's cannons ashore and made walls of earth to beat off attacks by Dutch warships. The British later built three forts there with some very special features. Two of the forts guarded each side of the narrow opening to St. John's Harbour with a thick chain connecting them that could be raised to keep enemy ships out.

Today, a row of nineteenth-century cannons stands among the fort ruins on Signal Hill, and one of them, "the noon gun,"

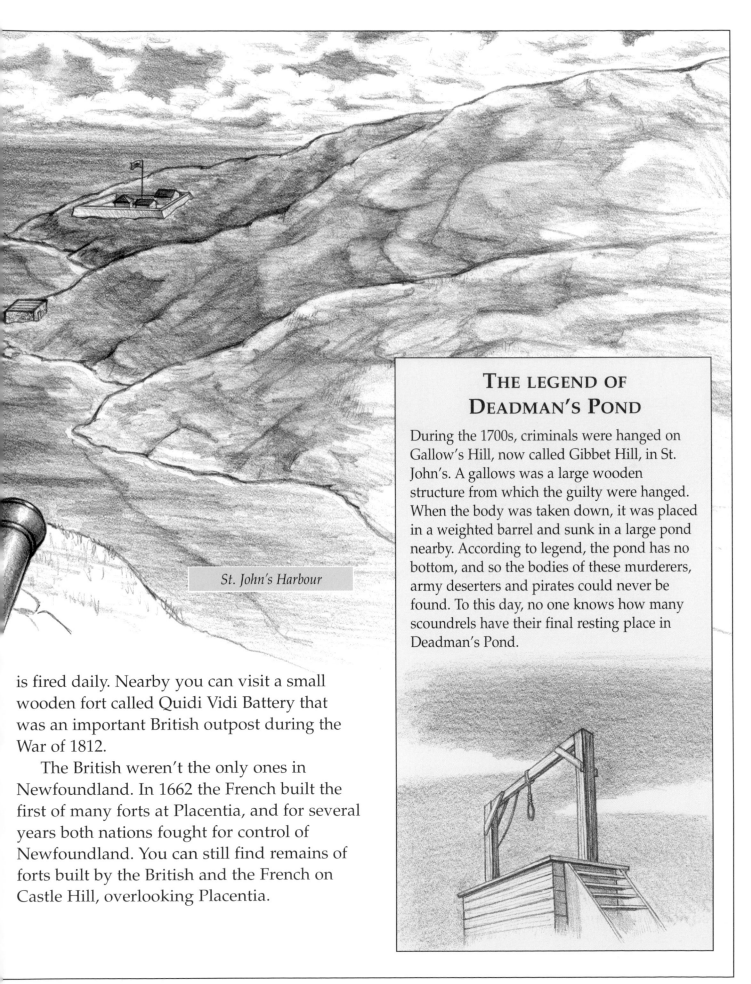

St. John's Harbour

THE LEGEND OF DEADMAN'S POND

During the 1700s, criminals were hanged on Gallow's Hill, now called Gibbet Hill, in St. John's. A gallows was a large wooden structure from which the guilty were hanged. When the body was taken down, it was placed in a weighted barrel and sunk in a large pond nearby. According to legend, the pond has no bottom, and so the bodies of these murderers, army deserters and pirates could never be found. To this day, no one knows how many scoundrels have their final resting place in Deadman's Pond.

is fired daily. Nearby you can visit a small wooden fort called Quidi Vidi Battery that was an important British outpost during the War of 1812.

The British weren't the only ones in Newfoundland. In 1662 the French built the first of many forts at Placentia, and for several years both nations fought for control of Newfoundland. You can still find remains of forts built by the British and the French on Castle Hill, overlooking Placentia.

CHAPTER THREE

MILITARY FORTS

Military forts were always built for one reason — to claim and guard territory. That was also the job of the soldiers who lived in these forts, and they spent most of their time preparing their forts for attacks by invaders. Military forts were built on high ground so soldiers could have a good view of any approaching enemies. They were built near lakes and rivers so supplies of food and weapons could be shipped in easily.

Some military forts are haunted. Fort Henry in Kingston, Ontario, is still visited by the ghost of a soldier who was hanged for leading an American invasion into Canada. If you go to Fort Henry, you might see him entering an officer's room. Follow him and he disappears, but you can feel an eerie chill. This is the room where he spent his last night, writing his will with his lawyer, John A. Macdonald — who would later become Canada's first prime minister.

Fort Henry

No-frills forts

Blockhouses were forts specially designed for North America, and they were the most common type of military fort in Canada. Why? Because they were simple to build and could be constructed quickly. A typical blockhouse was made of squared logs with an upper storey larger than the lower one. There were openings on all four sides as well as around the edges of the floor of the upper storey so soldiers could shoot at attackers. Sometimes the lower storey was built of stone to make it stronger. When a blockhouse was built inside the walls of a larger fort, it was like having a fort within a fort. Blockhouses were built from logs or stones — whatever was nearby and free.

Once there were dozens of blockhouses, from Fort Edward in Windsor, Nova Scotia, to Nanaimo Bastion on Vancouver Island. Most were built during the War of 1812 to defend Canada from an American invasion. Some were as small as St. Andrews Blockhouse in New Brunswick, where three men lived. Others were as large as the stone blockhouse that housed 60 soldiers, 22 women and 48 children at Fort Wellington in Prescott, Ontario. Today, that many people would fill a whole apartment building, but life in a blockhouse was much more cramped because everyone lived in one large room. Military forts were built for defence, not comfort!

You'll need

• two 71 cm x 56 cm (28 in. x 22 in.) sheets of bristol board

• brown, grey, black and white paint and a paintbrush

• scissors, masking tape

1. Cut four pieces of bristol board 20 cm x 10 cm (8 in. x 4 in.) and tape the short sides together to form an open box. This is the first storey of your blockhouse.

2. Make a similar box using four 24 cm x 10 cm (9 1/2 in. x 4 in.) pieces of bristol board.

3. Cut a 24 cm x 24 cm (9 1/2 in. x 9 1/2 in.) bristol-board floor and tape it to the larger box. This is the overhanging second storey.

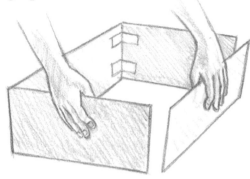

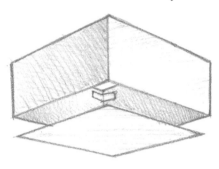

4. Tape the second storey on top of the first.

5. For the roof, cut four 24 cm x 24 cm x 24 cm (9 1/2 in. x 9 1/2 in. x 9 1/2 in.) cardboard triangles and tape them together to form a pyramid. Tape the roof on the second storey.

6. Paint your whole structure brown if you want a wooden blockhouse, or paint the top storey brown and the first storey grey if that part is supposed to be stone.

7. When the paint is dry, paint on the door, the openings for the soldiers' guns and lines between the logs or stones of the walls. Add details around your blockhouse such as bushes made from evergreen twigs stuck in Plasticine.

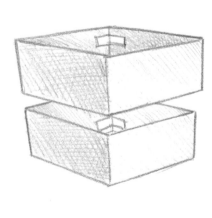

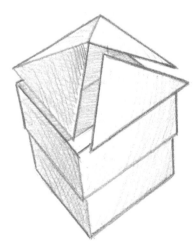

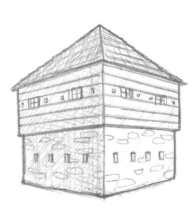

Recycled forts

Fort Lennox

When attacking armies captured forts, they often rebuilt them to suit their own needs. They sometimes changed the fort's name, too. For example, Fort Beauséjour on the Bay of Fundy in New Brunswick became Fort Cumberland when the British captured it from the French in 1755.

Fort Lennox, south of Montreal, was recycled three times in its long history. First the French built a wooden fort in 1759 on the "Ile aux Noix" (Island of Nuts) that one of their soldiers had rented for "a bag of nuts." The British captured it in 1760 and left it in ruins. Then, the Americans used the ruined fort as a base for an attack on Montreal in 1775. After the Americans retreated, the British built a larger fort on the site. It included a shipyard to repair ships for the navy, stone buildings such as the powder magazine (see next page) and a star-shaped moat.

If you were a soldier in those days, you might have helped rebuild old forts to bring them up-to-date with "modern" military technology. As more accurate rifles and cannons were invented, it became necessary to construct sturdier forts with earth-banked walls, deep ditches and buildings of stone rather than wood.

MAKE A POWDER MAGAZINE

The powder magazine was a small building that held all the fort's ammunition. Its thick stone walls and tin roof protected the ammunition from enemy cannon fire. The magazine had to have air vents so that dampness from the stone wouldn't wet the powder and make it useless. To prevent sparks that could set off the ammunition, wooden pegs were used instead of nails, and locks and door handles were made of non-sparking copper instead of iron.

You'll need
- a small box, approximately 8 cm wide x 8 cm high x 12 cm long (3 in. x 3 in. x 5 in.)
- a small brass paper fastener
- brown and grey Plasticine or other modelling clay and a pencil
- a piece of black construction paper
- scissors, tape

1. Place the box open side down and draw an arched doorway in the middle of one side. The door should be about 6 cm (2½ in.) high and 3 cm (1¼ in.) wide. Cut along one side and the top, then fold the door open along the other side.

2. For the door handle, poke a paper fastener through the door and bend its ends out, as shown, so the door will stay closed when the knob is turned.

3. Cut one small ventilation slit on each of the other three walls, as shown.

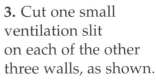

4. Cover the door of your powder magazine with brown clay. Cover the rest of it with grey clay. Use the point of a pencil to make lines in the clay to look like bricks.

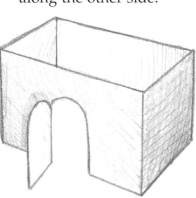

5. For the roof, cut a piece of construction paper 12 cm long x 10 cm wide (5 in. x 4 in.). Fold it in half lengthwise. Then cut two triangles 8 cm x 5 cm x 5 cm (3 in. x 2 in. x 2 in.) and tape them to the ends of the roof.

Trusty muskets ...

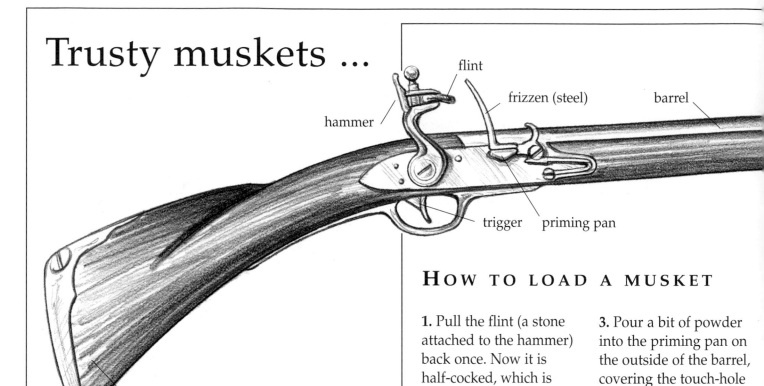

flint

frizzen (steel)

barrel

hammer

trigger   priming pan

butt

It is 1750, and 16-year-old François Dubois has already been a soldier for two years. His musket is his most prized possession, and he is proud to be guarding Fort Chambly on the Richelieu River in Quebec. It looks like a castle with its high walls of stone and bastions at each of its four corners. François's job is to watch from the fort's enclosed lookout towers (called bartizans) for approaching Iroquois war canoes or invading British soldiers. Like all military forts, Fort Chambly has loopholes — narrow openings that allow François to shoot at attackers without being hit. His flint-lock musket is heavy, it seldom hits its target and loading it is complicated.

HOW TO LOAD A MUSKET

1. Pull the flint (a stone attached to the hammer) back once. Now it is half-cocked, which is the safety position, and will not fire.

3. Pour a bit of powder into the priming pan on the outside of the barrel, covering the touch-hole that connects with the barrel's inside.

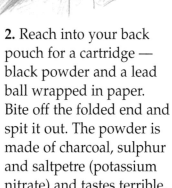

2. Reach into your back pouch for a cartridge — black powder and a lead ball wrapped in paper. Bite off the folded end and spit it out. The powder is made of charcoal, sulphur and saltpetre (potassium nitrate) and tastes terrible.

4. Pull the frizzen (steel that the flint will strike) closed over the pan.

ram rod

5. Put the butt of the musket down by your left foot and pour the rest of the gunpowder down the barrel. Crumple the paper around the lead ball and put it in too.

6. Push down twice with the ramrod to force the ball down the barrel of the musket.

7. Pull the flint back all the way to be fully cocked; now it's in the fire position.

8. Put the musket against your right shoulder, point it at your target and pull the trigger. This will cause the flint to strike the steel and a spark will fall into the pan.

9. Be careful not to flinch as the powder in the pan catches fire with a sizzle and a flash. The powder inside the barrel ignites through the touch-hole.

10. The powder explodes with a puff of smoke and sends the lead ball approximately 100 m (330 ft.), about the length of a football field. This whole process would take a trained soldier like François about half a minute.

... and mighty cannons

At Fort George in Niagara-on-the-Lake, Ontario, Corporal Herbert Brown peers through a telescope at the walls of the American Fort Niagara across the river. Fort Niagara had once been a British fort, but after the American Revolution in 1776 it lay on the American side of the new border between the United States and Canada. The British built Fort George in 1796 to replace Fort Niagara because they suspected the Americans still wanted to take over more British territory.

British military forts were planned and built to make the best use of their heavy artillery weapons — cannons — and to be strong enough to withstand enemy cannon fire. Herbert is a member of an artillery regiment, which means he is especially trained to load, aim and fire the fort's cannons. The cannon that Herbert works on is called a "12 pounder" because it fires cannon balls that weigh 12 pounds (5.5 kg). It is well placed on a high bastion so Herbert and the six other gunners in his squad can send cannon balls right across the river into Fort Niagara, 1.2 km (¾ mi.) away.

Herbert and the other gunners often practise loading and firing the cannon so they can do it very quickly during battle. One gunner cleans the cannon barrel and

Fort George

another wipes it with a wet sponge so that no sparks will cause an explosion at the wrong time. Then a bag of gunpowder — the cartridge — is loaded into the barrel and rammed down under the small hole where the wick will be placed. Then a gunner puts in the shot (see sidebar). The cartridge is punctured by ramming a metal spike down the wick hole, and the wick is inserted. Gunpowder burns rapidly and forms gases that expand quickly, so when the wick is lit, the shot is forced out of the cannon's mouth with a sudden burst of noise and smoke.

DEADLY CHOICES: DIFFERENT TYPES OF SHOT

Cannons didn't just fire solid cannon balls. There were many different types of ammunition that gunners like Herbert could use in battle.

"Hot shot" was cannon balls that were heated in portable ovens to such a high temperature that they would set fire to wooden targets, such as ships or palisades.

"Chain shot" was two cannon balls joined together by heavy chain links. It could rip sails and topple masts when fired at ships.

"Canister shot" was a container the size of a large juice can that was filled with musket balls that would scatter and hit many targets.

If soldiers ran out of musket balls, they would fill the canisters with stones, nails, glass or even kitchen cutlery. A flying fork in an enemy's eye could be just as effective as a musket wound.

Exploding cannon balls were launched high in the air by short-barrelled cannons called mortars or howitzers. Mortars fired shot in an arc rather than straight ahead and so could lob ammunition up over fort walls. It would then explode and shower the enemy with pieces of metal called shrapnel.

Battle tactics

Have you ever played a game of checkers or chess? It's a bit like fighting a battle because you use some of your playing pieces to capture your opponent's pieces. When you choose a certain piece to move, you are using a battle tactic to help you win the game.

Military commanders had a number of battle tactics to help them save their fort or capture other forts. The usual tactic used to capture a well-defended fort was a siege. This would work only if the attackers had enough soldiers to surround the fort and enough ammunition and food to outlast the supplies that were in the fort. This tactic worked for the British against the French at the Fortress of Louisbourg in 1745, but not against the Americans at Fort Erie, Ontario, in 1814 because they could not completely cut Fort Erie off from American supply ships.

A more original tactic was used by the Ojibway in 1763 to capture Fort Michilimackinac in Michigan from the British. The warriors distracted the sentries by playing lacrosse just outside the fort, then suddenly rushed through the gates with their weapons.

Fort Michilimackinac

34

Powder Magazine, Fort York

Another way to win is to scare the enemy. When the British General Brock attacked Fort Detroit during the War of 1812, he put Aboriginal warriors at the front of his army. The Americans were so afraid of the warriors that they surrendered.

A Canadian militia leader in the War of 1812 tricked the American attackers at Chateauguay, Quebec, to keep them from invading Montreal. He had his men march within sight of the Americans, then double back and march by a second time to make it seem as though he had a larger army.

Sometimes the best tactic was not to fight at all, and so commanders would order their soldiers to retreat. If their fort was being captured, their last tactic might be to prevent ammunition from falling into the enemies' hands. Just before Fort York (in present-day Toronto) was captured in 1813, its defenders retreated and blew up the powder magazine. That not only used up the gunpowder but it also killed or wounded 250 invading Americans and their leader.

Life for a soldier

Soldiers in some Canadian forts during the 1800s had a life of parties and good food, while others had to put up with little money and a cold bunkhouse. Why were some so lucky? It all depended on their army rank, and that depended on whether they'd been rich or poor before they joined the army. Most common soldiers joined up because they were homeless and out of work. In the army they were at least fed and clothed — even if the bread was hard, the boiled beef sometimes rotten and the uniform hot and scratchy.

Common soldiers were paid 12 cents a day, but 4 cents was subtracted for food and clothing. There was very little free time because the officers ordered them to do chores and endless military drills. Disobedience brought harsh punishments, such as whipping, branding and even death.

An officer had a much easier life. As the son of a rich family, he would have bought his rank as officer. His army pay was much higher than a common soldier's. Officers had their own rooms at the fort and enjoyed fancy dinners, dances, card parties, fishing and hunting — even painting or fossil collecting.

British soldiers were known as the "redcoats" because all the foot-soldiers (infantry) wore scarlet wool jackets. The uniforms of the artillery soldiers were dark blue to hide the black powder marks that came from working around the cannons. On his head, a British soldier wore a "shako," the stiff black hat that was designed to make him seem taller and more frightening to the enemy.

You'll need

• a 71 cm x 56 cm (28 in. x 22 in.) sheet of black bristol board

• aluminum foil

• a sheet of white tissue paper

• tape measure, scissors, clear tape, glue

1. Measure the circumference of your head with the tape measure.

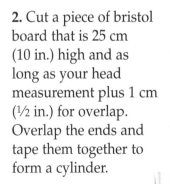

2. Cut a piece of bristol board that is 25 cm (10 in.) high and as long as your head measurement plus 1 cm (½ in.) for overlap. Overlap the ends and tape them together to form a cylinder.

3. Use the cylinder as a guide to cut a circle for the top of your hat and a crescent shape for the visor that shields your eyes from the sun. Tape both onto the hat.

4. Cut an oval 10 cm x 5 cm (4 in. x 2 in.) from bristol board. Cover it with foil to be your army badge and glue it above the visor.

5. To make a pompom, crumple the tissue paper into a tight ball and glue it above the badge.

Life for a fort family

What was it like to live in a military fort in the 1800s? If your father was an officer, your home would have been comfortable rooms or even a well-furnished house within the fort walls. But if your father was one of the common soldiers who was allowed to have his family live at the fort (very few were able to), you lived in the crowded soldiers' barracks. This was a common room for sleeping, eating, working and playing.

For a bit of privacy, your mother would have hung a blanket around the bed you shared with your parents each night. When you grew too big to sleep with them, you would have to sleep on a mat under the bed. Or if you found out which soldier was on guard duty that night and you were quick, you might be lucky enough to claim his bed.

You were fed the same food as the soldiers, but only one-quarter the amount. Your mother received half of a soldier's food ration. To make a little money, she would wash clothes, sew or knit for the men. You and the other children were expected to help with chores, as well as attend school in the fort or in the town it guarded.

THE THREE SCHOOLS AT FORT HENRY

Before 1850, education was only for the rich. In fact, common soldiers were not allowed to read books or newspapers in case they picked up rebellious ideas. But gradually it became desirable to have soldiers who could read their orders. In Fort Henry in Kingston, Ontario, there were three schools: one for the soldiers who had never learned to read and write, one for their children (boys and girls up to age 12) and another for the older boys who would likely have army careers. Teenaged girls were taught housekeeping by their mothers.

In their spare time, kids played with wooden dolls or lead soldiers, enjoyed hopscotch or marbles, or made toys like the one below.

MAKE A FORT TOY: CUP-ON-A-STICK

For this game, eighteenth-century kids used a cup made from wood or bark.

You'll need
• a paper cup
• a piece of string 35 cm (14 in.) long
• a stick 30 cm (12 in.) long
• scissors

1. With the scissors, poke a small hole in the bottom of the cup.

2. Tie one end of the string to one end of the stick.

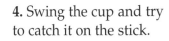

3. Push the other end of the string through the hole in the cup and tie a knot so the string won't slip out.

4. Swing the cup and try to catch it on the stick.

CHAPTER FOUR

TRADING FORTS

Trading forts — sometimes called posts, houses or factories — protected the first stores in Canada. They came in all shapes and sizes, from the thick stone walls of Lower Fort Garry in Manitoba, to the wooden palisades of Fort St. James in British Columbia. Aboriginal people brought furs and sometimes fish or dried fruit to these forts to trade for blankets, axes and guns.

From the 1760s to the mid-1800s, traders from the North West and Hudson's Bay Companies travelled farther into the Canadian northwest, seeking more furs. These men quickly built simple forts to protect their territory, as well as to survive in the wilderness.

In this chapter you will find out about Canada's first fast food, a voyageur game and how to make fruit roll-ups.

Lower Fort Garry

Forts of the voyageurs

Fort William

If you were young, strong, male, not too tall and willing to work 18 hours a day, eat bad food and sleep under a canoe, you could have been a voyageur for the North West Company at Fort William, Ontario. There were two groups of voyageurs. If you delivered supplies to Fort William and took furs back to Montreal, you were known as a "pork eater" because every meal you ate on the trip would be pork, peas and porridge. If you brought in furs to Fort William from northern wilderness outposts and took back supplies for more trading, you were called an *homme du nord*, which means man of the north.

In early July, from 1803 until 1821, sentries at Fort William would fire muskets and cannons to signal the arrival of hundreds of canoes — the beginning of the annual Rendezvous. For the rest of that month, Fort William would bustle with activity as furs were counted and trade goods, such as knives, kettles, tobacco and blankets, were packed to be sent back to the northern fur posts for the next fur-trading season.

At night in the Grand Hall of the fort there would be feasting and dancing, but only for the partners and clerks of the North West Company. The voyageurs camped outside the fort, with the pork eaters from Montreal on one side and the *hommes du nord* on the other. After a night of drinking and fighting, many would end up in the *pot au beurre* — the nickname given to Fort William's jail, which was also an outhouse.

FORT-TO-FORT TRANSPORT

In the 1700s and 1800s, lakes and rivers were the highways that connected forts. Like transport trucks on super highways today, large freighter canoes called *canots du maître* were used on major waterways. Each canoe could carry 4000 kg (8820 lb.) of supplies — the equivalent of 440 cases of cans of soda pop — and needed at least 12 voyageurs to paddle it.

On narrower rivers, smaller canoes called *canots du nord* transported supplies in the same way we use smaller delivery vans on city streets. These smaller canoes needed only two paddlers and could be carried when the voyageurs had to portage around rapids or between rivers.

VOYAGEUR WRESTLING

Voyageurs were tough guys who were always trying to prove their strength by wrestling or fighting. You can try a fun version of voyageur wrestling with a friend. Find a log big enough for you both to stand on. Each of you stand at opposite ends of the log with one arm behind your back. Take turns rocking the log to see which one of you can stay on the longest.

Northern outposts

Stuart Fraser curses that day in 1810 when he signed on with the North West Company to run their trading post, Rocky Mountain House in Alberta. His room is so cold that his ink has frozen and the inside log walls are covered with frost. The storm last night blew down part of the wooden palisade surrounding the post, but he and his three traders are too cold and hungry to repair it. The last of their dried meat, called pemmican, is gone and unless they have some luck hunting, the only things left to eat are their leather shoes.

Life at all northern outposts was difficult. The hard winters meant constant work just to stay warm and fed. Through all of this the traders of the North West Company and the Hudson's Bay Company were trying to bring in as many furs as possible. The daily routine in a North West Company fort such as Fort George in Alberta or Fort St. James in British Columbia centred around fur trading, gathering wood and hunting for food. Any free time was often spent drinking and gambling.

Hudson's Bay Company forts, on the other hand, such as York Factory in Manitoba or Cumberland House in Saskatchewan, were highly disciplined. The chief factor, the company man in charge, was usually an ex-navy officer, and he ran his fort as efficiently as if he was still captain of a ship. At York Factory, work shifts and mealtimes were announced by naval bells. All employees were required to keep careful records of every transaction. Perhaps that's why the Hudson's Bay Company stores are still in business today.

PEMMICAN

Dried buffalo meat mixed with animal fat was Canada's first fast food. Long-lasting, easily packaged and high in energy, pemmican became the main food in forts. During the long winters when fresh food could not be found, it meant the difference between life and death to those who had to stay in northern outposts. Thousands of bags of pemmican were prepared each year, mostly by Aboriginal women. The main purpose of some forts, such as Fort Carlton in Saskatchewan, was to produce pemmican and transport it to other forts.

BANNOCK

If you were lucky, you might have had some bannock to eat with your pemmican.

You'll need
- 750 mL (3 c.) all-purpose flour
- 15 mL (1 tbsp.) baking powder
- 7 mL (1½ tsp.) salt
- 25 mL (2 tbsp.) sugar (optional)
- 375 mL (1½ c.) water
- large mixing bowl, fork, greased pie plate

1. Mix flour, baking powder, salt and sugar together in the bowl.

2. Add the water all at once and stir until all the ingredients are well blended.

3. Spread the dough in the pie plate. Bake in a preheated oven at 220°C (425°F) for 20 minutes.

4. Serve your bannock warm with butter and jam.

The company store

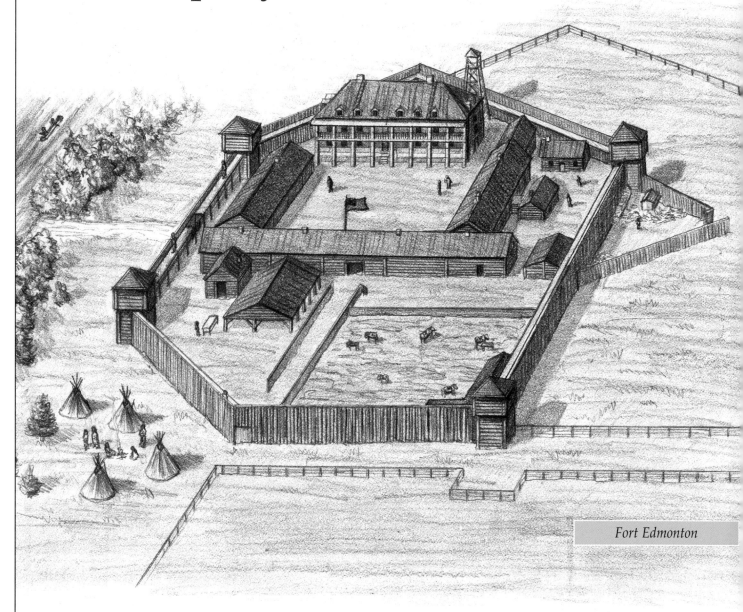

Fort Edmonton

Today an amusement park attracts shoppers to the West Edmonton Mall, but in the 1830s it was the paintings and decorations in Fort Edmonton that drew Aboriginal people to trade furs. Sitting high on a bluff overlooking the Saskatchewan River, this Hudson's Bay Company fort was an impressive sight. Its 6 m (20 ft.) high palisade of squared logs surrounded an area about the size of a baseball field. Cannons were mounted on the corner bastions. Fort Edmonton's chief factor lived in the "Big House," a three-storey house with a balcony and the first glass windows in the West. Meanwhile, his clerks slept in a bunkhouse with only parchment skin to cover the windows. For the next 20 years, Fort Edmonton was to be one of the Hudson Bay Company's most important western posts.

"THE LITTLE EMPEROR" SIR GEORGE SIMPSON

From 1821 until 1860 George Simpson ruled the Hudson's Bay Company. He helped bring about the union of the two most powerful fur companies: the Hudson's Bay Company and the North West Company. As governor of the company, Sir George controlled fur trading and exploration in Rupert's Land — an area including parts of Alberta, Saskatchewan, Ontario, Quebec, the Northwest Territories and all of Manitoba.

Sir George's short height and bossy manner earned him the nickname "Little Emperor." His employees tried to get along well with him because he kept a "Book of Servants' Characters" in which he would write down his feelings about you. This would determine whether you got a raise in pay or were thrown in the fort jail.

Always on the go travelling by canoe and horseback, Sir George liked to make surprise visits to the forts to check on business. Wearing his beaver top hat and fancy black coat and with his Scottish bagpiper announcing his arrival, the Little Emperor always attracted a great deal of attention.

ARCHAEOLOGY DETECTIVE

All the artifacts pictured below are items you could have found in a fur-trading fort in the early 1800s. Can you match the pictures with the descriptions?

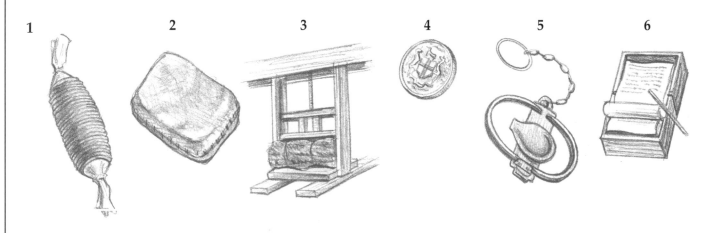

1 2 3 4 5 6

A. Fur press (it flattened furs for easy packing and transport)

B. Tobacco carrot (tobacco leaves that were compressed and could be smoked in a pipe)

C. A trading token known as a Made-Beaver

D. Pemmican (dried buffalo meat and animal fat packed in a bag)

E. Copy machine from Fort William

F. Beaver trap

(Answers page 63.)

Trading rituals

When you and a friend trade sports cards, comics or marbles, you are bartering. Instead of giving each other money, you decide how much the things you are trading are worth to each of you. In 1815 the Hudson's Bay Company forts used a form of bartering with Aboriginal people. Rather than using money, they used a token they called a Made-Beaver (see page 47). Aboriginal people were given one Made-Beaver for every perfect beaver pelt. Other animal pelts were compared with beavers. For instance, three fox skins might be worth one Made-Beaver. At Fort George in Alberta, a gun could have been traded for 14 Made-Beavers or a blanket for 6. The number of skins needed for a trade was decided by the company, and the rates went up or down depending on how many furs were available.

If you worked at a major fur-trading fort, you looked forward to the yearly trading time (usually in June or July) and the arrival of Aboriginal people with their furs. No trading began until certain ceremonies were performed. First, the Aboriginal chief was given a red wool coat with brass buttons as a sign of his importance, as well as gifts of alcohol and tobacco. There were long speeches made by both Aboriginal chiefs and officers of the fort, and then everyone joined in the smoking of a peace pipe. Finally, there was a party, with feasting and celebrating

ALL THE RAGE

Fur has always been valued for its warmth, but by the 1600s it had become a status symbol in Europe. Just as you want certain running shoes or baseball caps, everyone in Europe wanted a beaver hat. Why beaver? The beaver pelt could be made into various shapes, it didn't wear out and it was waterproof. The hats were so valuable that owners would write in their will who in the family should inherit them. As a result of this high demand, traders explored deeper and deeper into Canada looking for more furs.

going on all night. The next morning the Aboriginal people would bring out their furs to begin trading.

The actual trading usually took place at a small window. At Fort Edmonton, furs were pushed through a hole in the wall of the trading room and the trade goods were slid back. Each Aboriginal person brought in about a hundred pelts to trade for hatchets, ice chisels, knives, files, flints, kettles, beads and tobacco. Deciding on items could take days — there was no impulse shopping — and if a hunter felt his pelts were not given good value, he would threaten to take them elsewhere.

Guarding the Grease Trail

Kitwanga Fort

Aboriginal peoples built many forts along the trade routes between the coast and the interior of British Columbia. Along one important route, the Grease Trail — it was called this because one of the main trade items carried along it was fish oil — stood Kitwanga Fort.

Over 200 years ago the Gitksan people built Kitwanga to protect them against raiding parties from other Nations. The fortress was a palisade of sharpened wooden stakes that surrounded five dwelling houses built on the top of a large hill known as Battle Hill. Some of the buildings extended over the edge of the hill and were held up on stilts.

For Kitwanga's defence, massive logs were held at the top of the hill by cedar ropes. At the sound of the sentry's horn, the ropes were cut and the logs rolled down, crushing the attackers. Trap doors in the floors of the buildings led to an escape tunnel under the palisade.

Today nothing remains of Kitwanga Fort. Sometime in the 1800s it was burned to the ground. The descendants of those who escaped through the tunnel are still living nearby.

NEKT AND "STRIKE ONLY ONCE"

Legend has it that Nekt, a chief of Kitwanga, killed a grizzly bear and made a suit of armour for himself by lining the bearskin with thin pieces of rock. This protected him from arrows and clubs. Wearing his armour and a large wooden helmet and carrying a "magic club" called Strike Only Once, he would have seemed impossible to defeat. But his magic couldn't save him from the power of guns. One legend has it that a shot from the first gun brought into his valley killed him.

THE ORIGINAL FRUIT ROLL-UP

Dried fruit was an important trade item and food for the Aboriginal peoples of the West Coast. The women collected the fruit and dried it over an open fire. It was then rolled onto sticks to be stored. You can make your own dried fruit roll-ups.

You'll need

• 500 mL (2 c.) hulled strawberries, fresh or frozen (thawed)

• 15 mL (1 tbsp.) sugar

• blender, baking sheet with an edge, plastic wrap, scissors

1. Blend berries and sugar in the blender for 20 seconds or until all lumps are gone and you have a thick liquid.

2. Cover the bottom and edges of the baking sheet with plastic wrap.

3. Pour the blended berries in an even layer onto the sheet.

4. Put the tray on the middle rack of the oven. Set the oven at the lowest temperature possible. It will take about four hours for the fruit to dry. Fruit roll-ups are done when they look dry but are still red. (You may have to leave the oven door open slightly.)

5. When the fruit is dry, tip it out of the baking sheet and peel the plastic off. Cut the fruit into strips with scissors, then roll up the strips.

CHAPTER FIVE

FORTS GO WEST

Western forts were different from the forts in the east. They were built not to claim and guard land but to give settlers a base for their new life. Outlaws who traded in whiskey built forts with names such as Whoop-Up. The Mounties set up Fort Walsh, Fort Calgary and others to provide law and order. Fur-trading forts, such as Fort Langley, became the first shopping centres, selling supplies to gold seekers.

Frontier forts were rough and built in a hurry from whatever material was available. But with no other buildings for hundreds of miles, they became important places for new settlers to find help and company.

Read on and find out what life was like for the North-West Mounted Police and how you can make a western fort.

Fort Langley

Whiskey forts

Fort Whoop-up

Whiskey forts and posts were built mainly by American traders who were looking for adventure and a chance to make money. Men with names such as Joe Kipp, J.J. Healy and Liver Eating Johnson made thousands of dollars by trading alcohol to the Blackfoot people for buffalo robes and other furs.

More than 50 whiskey forts were built across southern Alberta and Saskatchewan between 1869 and 1874. The first, largest and most important became known as Fort Whoop-Up. It had a squared timber stockade with two bastions and each bastion was mounted with a brass cannon and a mountain howitzer, as well as having loopholes for rifles. A small door built into the main gate was opened to allow only a few Blackfoot traders in at a time. They traded in what was called the "Indian Room," where they exchanged their furs for rifles, cloth, sugar and whiskey.

A massacre led to the end of the whiskey forts. In 1873 two groups — non-Aboriginal wolf hunters and Assiniboine — were camped at a whiskey fort called Farwell's Trading Post in the Cypress Hills of Saskatchewan. After an argument over a stolen horse, the "wolfers" attacked the Assiniboine camp and killed more than 20 men, women and children. This massacre was one of the reasons why in 1874 the government formed the North-West Mounted Police (later renamed the Royal Canadian Mounted Police, or RCMP) to march out west in their bright red jackets and close down the whiskey forts.

BUILD A WESTERN FORT

You'll need

• an open box 8 cm (3 in.) high, 30 cm (12 in.) wide and 40 cm (16 in.) long (the bottom of a soda-pop case works well)

• 250 Popsicle sticks (available at craft stores)

• 4 tall boxes, each about 8 cm x 8 cm x 25 cm (3 in. x 3 in. x 10 in.)

• small boxes for fort buildings

• scissors, glue, paint and a paintbrush

1. Place the large box open side up. Cut a line down the middle of one of the long sides. On both sides of the line, cut a 5 cm (2 in.) long line along the base of the box, as shown. Fold back the cardboard to make the gates.

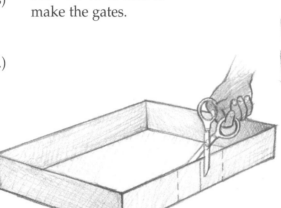

3. Glue one of the four tall boxes upright into each of the corners for bastions. Paint them or cover them with Popsicle sticks.

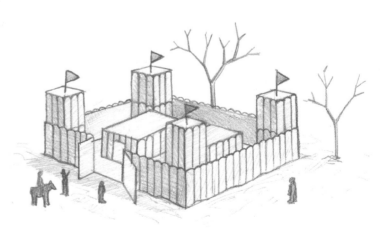

4. Paint the smaller boxes to look like fort buildings and place them inside the palisade.

5. Add whatever details you like according to what you see in the illustration on pages 52 or 54.

2. Glue Popsicle sticks upright onto the outside of all four sides, including the gate.

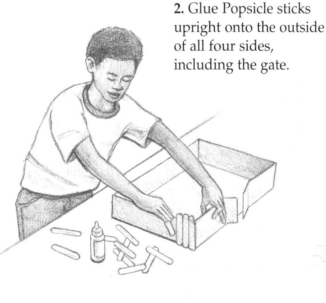

The Mounties take charge

Fort Macleod,
Nov. 24, 1874.

Dear Mother and Father,

I'm sorry that it's been three months since my last letter but the march from Lower Fort Garry to Fort Whoop-Up was a nightmare. When we marched out, so proud to be the first troops of the North-West Mounted Police, we didn't know the problems that were ahead. The blackflies drove the men and horses crazy. Then we ran out of food except for flour and potatoes. My boots wore out and I had to rip the sleeves from my uniform and tie them around my feet.

We got lost when we reached the Cypress Hills, but luckily Inspector Macleod found a guide called Jerry Potts. When I first saw him I was doubtful that he could help us. His clothes were part-Aboriginal and part-European and he was covered in old battle scars, but without a map or compass he led us straight to Fort Whoop-Up.

You needn't have worried, Mother, about me fighting because when those whiskey traders heard the Mounties were coming they fled.

With the cold weather coming we had to work night and day to build our first fort. It's called Fort Macleod after our leader. It doesn't look like much, just a square wooden stockade with a building on the inside of each wall. We had to build the stables for the horses before we could make our own barracks.

If you can send any money that would help because my pay of 75 cents a day doesn't buy much out here. I may be moved out to help build the next fort. The North-West Mounted Police want to build a number of forts to make the West safe for settlers.

Your loving son,
John

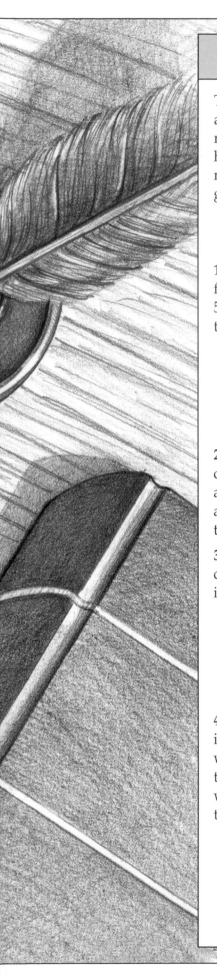

LETTER WRITING WITH A QUILL PEN

The only way you could receive news at a North-West Mounted Police fort was by mail. Many hours were spent writing letters home and keeping diaries. To write, you might have used a feather from a turkey or goose called a quill.

You'll need
- large feathers (available at craft stores)
- scissors
- calligraphy ink
- an adult helper

1. Cut the barbs from the bottom 5 cm (2 in.) of the quill.

2. Ask an adult to cut the quill on a slant to make a fine point at the tip, as shown.

3. Ask her to also cut a small slit in the tip.

4. Dip the point in the ink and try writing with it. You can vary the thickness of your writing by widening the slit in the point.

Changing forts

Belmont Battery at Fort Rodd Hill

By the early 1900s the West was settled and Canada had become a peaceful place to live. Forts were no longer needed for protection. As cities grew around them, the old forts were abandoned, torn down or put to other uses. Lower Fort Garry near Winnipeg became an insane asylum and later a country club. The Halifax Citadel was used to imprison prisoners-of-war in World War I. Fort Malden, near Windsor, Ontario, was converted to a lumber mill.

Forts became out-of-date when fighter planes, submarines and spy satellites were invented. Fort Rodd Hill near Victoria was the last fort to be built in Canada and the last to have soldiers on duty. Its underground bunkers and "disappearing guns" were ready for combat during both world wars and soldiers were stationed there until 1957.

Fort Langley near Vancouver is a good example of how some forts changed over the years. It was built in 1827 as a fur-trading fort for the Hudson's Bay Company. When furs fell out of fashion, the fort developed other ways to stay in business. Instead of furs, Aboriginal people traded salmon, which was shipped as far away as Hawaii. Cranberries were traded and shipped to California, and the fort also started a dairy farm. It was at Fort Langley in 1858 that British Columbia was declared a Crown colony and that same year the fort became famous as the starting point of the Fraser River gold rush. After the gold rush ended, the fort was abandoned. Today, Fort Langley has been restored to look as it did in the 1850s, and costumed guides show you what life was like then.

Forts are back in use today as places where you can see life as it was in early Canada. At many forts you can take part in special activities to learn what it was like to live in a fort.

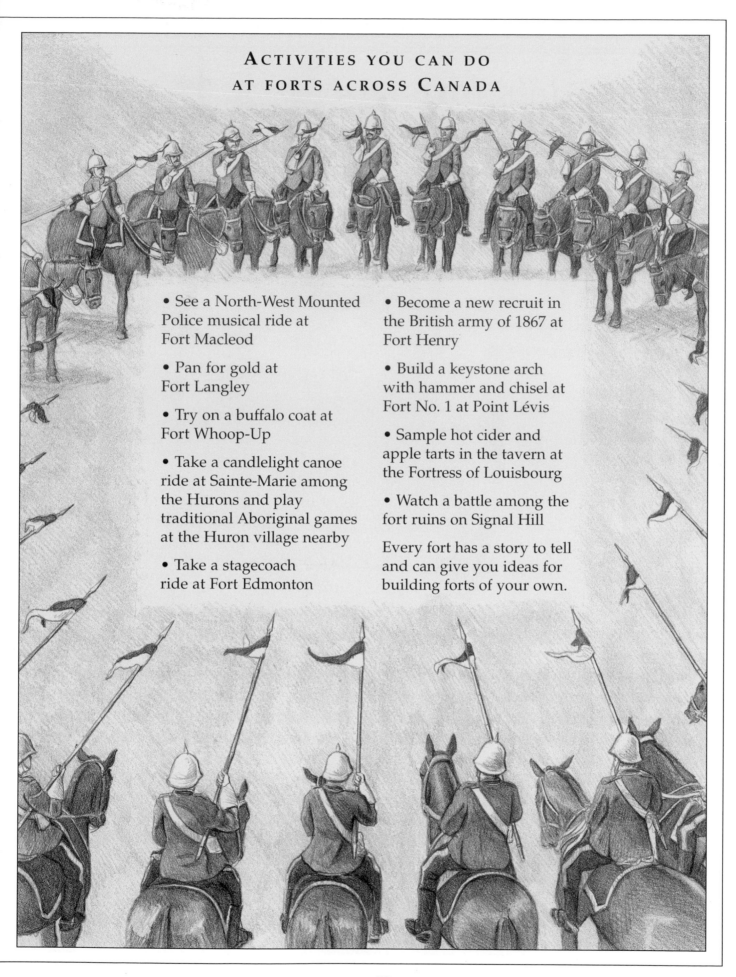

ACTIVITIES YOU CAN DO AT FORTS ACROSS CANADA

• See a North-West Mounted Police musical ride at Fort Macleod

• Pan for gold at Fort Langley

• Try on a buffalo coat at Fort Whoop-Up

• Take a candlelight canoe ride at Sainte-Marie among the Hurons and play traditional Aboriginal games at the Huron village nearby

• Take a stagecoach ride at Fort Edmonton

• Become a new recruit in the British army of 1867 at Fort Henry

• Build a keystone arch with hammer and chisel at Fort No. 1 at Point Lévis

• Sample hot cider and apple tarts in the tavern at the Fortress of Louisbourg

• Watch a battle among the fort ruins on Signal Hill

Every fort has a story to tell and can give you ideas for building forts of your own.

Canada's forts

You can find out more about many of the forts listed here by turning to the page numbers shown.

1. Fort Herchmer
2. Kitwanga Fort (p. 50-51)
3. Fort Rodd Hill (p. 58)
4. Nanaimo Bastion (p. 26)
5. Fort Langley (p. 52-53, 58-59)
6. Fort St. James (p. 40, 44)
7. Fort Kamloops
8. Fort Steele
9. Fort Macleod (p. 4, 56, 59)
10. Fort Whoop-Up (p. 52, 54, 56, 59)
11. Fort Calgary (p. 52)
12. Rocky Mountain House (p. 44)
13. Fort Edmonton (p. 46, 49, 59)
14. Fort George–Buckingham House (p. 44, 48)
15. Fort Walsh (p. 52)
16. Fort Battleford
17. Fort Carlton (p. 45)
18. Wood Mountain
19. Last Mountain House
20. Cumberland House (p. 44)
21. Fort la Reine
22. Lower Fort Garry (p. 40-41, 56, 58)
23. Prince of Wales Fort and Cape Merry
24. York Factory (p. 44)
25. Fort William (p. 42, 47)
26. Fort St. Joseph
27. Fort Malden (p. 58)
28. Prehistoric Indian Village
29. Fort Erie (p. 5, 34)
30. Fort George (p. 5, 32)
31. Crawford Lake
32. Fort York (p. 5, 35)
33. Huron Indian Village
34. Sainte-Marie among the Hurons (p. 12-13, 59)
35. Fort Kente
36. Murney Tower
37. Fort Henry (p. 5, 24, 39, 59)
38. Fort Frederick
39. Rideau Canal Blockhouses
40. Fort Wellington (p. 26)
41. Fort Témiscaming
42. Fort Lennox (p. 5, 28)
43. Blockhouse at Côteau-du-Lac
44. Old Fort
45. Fort Chambly (p. 30)
46. Quebec Citadel (p. 19)
47. Fort No. 1 at Point Lévis (p. 59)
48. Fort Ingall
49. St. Andrews Blockhouse (p. 26)
50. Fredericton Military Compound
51. Carleton Martello Tower (p. 4, 16)
52. Fort Beauséjour (p. 28)
53. Port Royal (p. 10)
54. Fort Anne
55. Fort Edward (p. 26)
56. Halifax Citadel (p. 16, 20, 58)
57. York Redoubt (p. 16)
58. Fort McNab
59. Prince of Wales Martello Tower (p. 16)
60. Fortress of Louisbourg (p. 14-16, 18-19, 34, 59)
61. Fort Amherst
62. Fort Edward Battery
63. Castle Hill (p. 23)
64. Signal Hill (p. 22, 59)
65. Quidi Vidi Battery (p. 23)

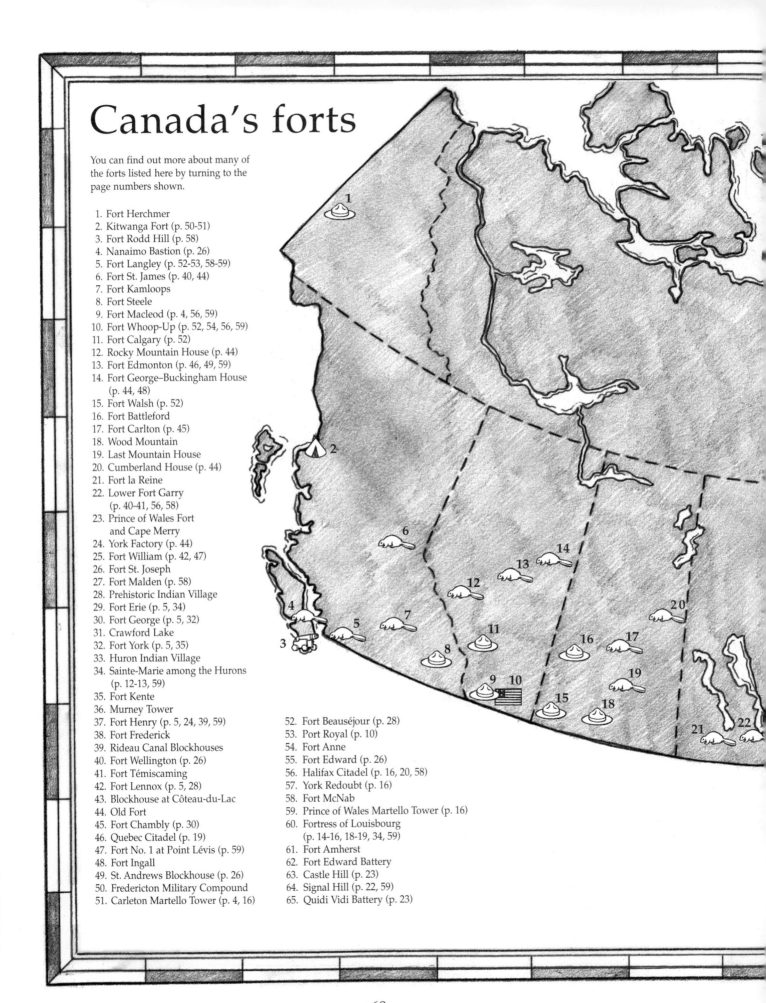

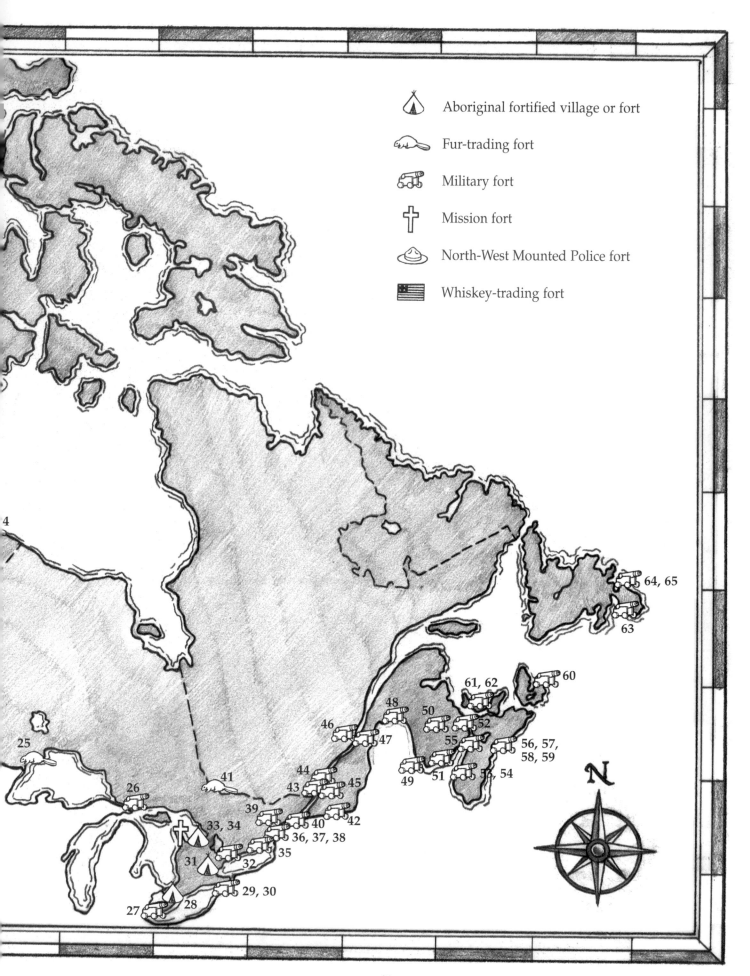

Aboriginal fortified village or fort

Fur-trading fort

Military fort

Mission fort

North-West Mounted Police fort

Whiskey-trading fort

Forts you can visit today

Name of fort	Location	Type of fort
Fort Herchmer	Dawson, YT	North-West Mounted Police fort
Kitwanga Fort	near Prince Rupert, BC	Aboriginal trading fort site and interpretive panels
Fort Rodd Hill	Victoria, BC	military fort
Nanaimo Bastion	Nanaimo, BC	fur-trading fort
Fort Langley	Langley, BC	fur-trading fort
Fort St. James	near Prince George, BC	fur-trading fort
Fort Kamloops	Kamloops, BC	fur-trading fort
Fort Steele	Fort Steele, BC	North-West Mounted Police fort
Fort Macleod	Lethbridge, AB	North-West Mounted Police fort
Fort Whoop-Up	Lethbridge, AB	whiskey-trading fort
Fort Calgary	Calgary, AB	North-West Mounted Police fort
Rocky Mountain House	Rocky Mountain House, AB	fur-trading fort
Fort Edmonton	Edmonton, AB	fur-trading fort
Fort George–Buckingham House	Elk Point, AB	fur-trading fort sites and interpretive centre
Fort Walsh	Maple Creek, SK	North-West Mounted Police fort
Fort Battleford	Battleford, SK	North-West Mounted Police fort
Fort Carlton	Prince Albert, SK	fur-trading fort
Wood Mountain	Moose Jaw, SK	North-West Mounted Police fort
Last Mountain House	Strasbourg, SK	fur-trading fort
Cumberland House	The Pas, MB	ruins of fur-trading fort
Fort la Reine	Portage la Prairie, MB	fur-trading fort

Name of fort	Location	Type of fort
Lower Fort Garry	Selkirk, MB	fur-trading fort
Prince of Wales Fort and Cape Merry	Churchill, MB	fur-trading forts
York Factory	York Factory, MB	fur-trading fort ruins
Fort William	Thunder Bay, ON	fur-trading fort
Fort St. Joseph	Sault Ste. Marie, ON	military fort ruins and interpretive centre
Fort Malden	Amherstburg, ON	military fort
Prehistoric Indian Village	London, ON	Aboriginal fortified village
Fort Erie	Fort Erie, ON	military fort
Fort George	Niagara-on-the-Lake, ON	military fort
Crawford Lake	Milton, ON	Aboriginal fortified village
Fort York	Toronto, ON	military fort
Huron Indian Village	Midland, ON	Aboriginal fortified village
Sainte-Marie among the Hurons	Midland, ON	mission fort
Fort Kente	Carrying Place, ON	military fort
Murney Tower	Kingston, ON	military fort
Fort Henry	Kingston, ON	military fort
Fort Frederick	Kingston, ON	military fort
Rideau Canal Blockhouses	Kingston Mills and Merrickville, ON	military forts
Fort Wellington	Prescott, ON	military fort
Fort Témiscaming	Ville-Marie, PQ	fur-trading fort
Fort Lennox	Île-aux-Noix, PQ	military fort
Blockhouse at Côteau-du-Lac	Côteau-du-Lac, PQ	military fort
Old Fort	Île Ste.-Hélène (Montreal), PQ	military fort
Fort Chambly	Chambly, PQ	military fort

Name of fort	Location	Type of fort
Quebec Citadel	Quebec City, PQ	military fort
Fort No. 1 at Point Lévis	Lauzon, PQ	military fort
Fort Ingall	Cabano, PQ	military fort
St. Andrews Blockhouse	St. Andrews-by-the-Sea, NB	military fort
Fredericton Military Compound	Fredericton, NB	military fort
Carleton Martello Tower	Saint John, NB	military fort
Fort Beauséjour	Sackville, NB	military fort
Port Royal	Annapolis Royal, NS	military fort
Fort Anne	Annapolis Royal, NS	military fort
Fort Edward	Windsor, NS	military fort
Halifax Citadel	Halifax, NS	military fort
York Redoubt	Halifax, NS	military fort
Fort McNab	McNab Island (Halifax), NS	military fort
Prince of Wales Martello Tower	Halifax, NS	military fort
Fortress of Louisbourg	Louisbourg, NS	military fort
Fort Amherst	Charlottetown, PE	military fort ruins and interpretive centre
Fort Edward Battery	Charlottetown, PE	military fort
Castle Hill	Placentia, NF	military fort ruins and interpretive centre
Signal Hill	St. John's, NF	military fort ruins and interpretive centre
Quidi Vidi Battery	St. John's, NF	military fort

GLOSSARY

barracks: living space for a large group of soldiers

bartizan: small wooden cabin overhanging a corner of a fort to give guards a wider view of the surrounding area

bastion: tower or platform at the corner of fort walls used as a lookout point

battery: a number of cannons that are fired together; also a platform for guns in a fort

citadel: a fortress in or near a city

embrassure: an opening wide enough to fire a cannon through

factor: an officer of a Hudson's Bay Company fort

loophole: a vertical slit through which a rifle or musket can be fired

magazine: a thick-walled stone building in which gunpowder and ammunition are stored

palisade/ stockade: a fort wall made of sharpened timbers dug into the ground

portage: a place on a canoe trip where the canoe must be carried, such as next to rapids or between two lakes

post: another name used for a trading fort; could also be called a house (e.g., Rocky Mountain House) or factory (e.g., York Factory)

rampart: a mound of earth outside the fort walls that protects the walls from cannon fire

sentry: a guard who looks out for enemies

siege: an attempt to take a fort by keeping it surrounded and under attack

stockade: see palisade

Answers for Archaeology Detective, page 47
1–B, 2–D, 3–A, 4–C, 5–F, 6–E.

INDEX